As the essences of Chi align Prahna energies emerge,
Then the Aura manifests as the souls Chakras converge,
And as our will gazes introspectively at its true nature,
The spirit connects skywards towards the infinite creator.

Then as Gaia's Lay-Line forces glow from below to above,
They resonate in our higher self the feelings of true love,
And as the high-sun illuminates your spirit in its golden beams,
Your higher power is reconnected to your hopes and your dreams.

Healed and empowered by the glory of living your inspirations,
As all true souls are borne of the energy and essence of creation,
For the 'DMT' 'Pineal Gland' 'Soul Nexus' reveals our past lives,
Connecting the higher self energies to the soul matrix inside.

Then through interstellar ascension we connect to the solar soul,
Harmonizing the vibration of our essence to the macrocosmic whole,
The infinite sentient wavelength captured in soul-glow spectrum,
A split-second of spiritual perfection in a Divine infinite introspection.

Other Books By Alan Garfoot

The Research Economy
The Infinity Theorem
Aspire To Inspire
Soul Nature
Spirit Vibe
Mind Shine
Divine Design
Empathic Energy
Telepathic Essence
Omnipathic Transcendence
Beyond The Portal
Dawn Of The Neomodern
Across The Wind Of Light
Spirit Of The Times
Soulific Lover
Sublime Dynamic 28

On Drugs:

Substance Rehabilitation & The Future Of International Psychoactive Policy

By Alan Garfoot Jnr. Cert. H.E.

On Drugs: Substance Rehabilitation & The Future Of International Psychoactive Policy

® The New World Thought Disorder

By Alan Garfoot Jnr. Cert. H.E.

Scunthorpe

(2023)

ISBN: 978-1-4477-8326-8

Printed By Lulu Press

On Drugs:

Substance Rehabilitation & The Future Of International Psychoactive Policy

By Alan Garfoot Jnr. Cert. H.E.

To Teiggs

'Legendary in every way!'

Contents:

Introduction:

It is obvious to the individuals concerned both all over the country and on the international level that the current illicit substance laws don't work or fit the modern requirements of today's society, especially the requirements and needs of the younger generations. Young individuals who are massively socialized into drug subculture from many different social strata and walks of life, from a relatively young age, through one route of mass-media subcultural identification or another.

Since the Misuse of Drugs Act was passed (1971) the Parsonian organic functioning of society, (Parsons, 1977) and the sociocultural nature of drug taking along with the inherent causation, of the collective identification of self within the subcultural context and the interpretation of the consequences of recreational drug use has definitely changed. The greater dynamics of society as a cultural and institutional organism has been undergoing constant change since the dominant drug law determining social policy white papers were passed, more than half a century ago.

It is essential now to our understanding how future drug laws are to be successfully implemented to highlight where the current drug laws have failed and cause more harm than good to the overall organic functioning of society. Done through comprehending the enabling and restricting consequences upon the social freedoms and autonomy of the citizens of our liberal, free and democratic society and our norms, ideals and values that constitute our way of life.

Accurately informed individuals are more enabled to make wiser and more intelligent choices and competent risk reducing decisions towards illicit drug use than are individuals blinded by ignorance, peer pressure or consensus swaying emotive and manipulative sensationalism in the cultural mass media. This book is an attempt to rid the subject of drug use of its shadows and illuminate those who wish to become aware, as to what the facts actually are.

The 'war on drugs' has definitely failed, its policy was intended to protect us from horrors of drug abuse and the consequences of taking drugs in the modern day; but it hasn't. In full fact the social issue of drug abuse is still being exasperated and magnified, as the problem it is attempting to solve is being pushed further and further underground into darker uncharted waters. Illegal drug use has in the modern globalising world become a billion dollar industry and it's a billion dollar industry in the hands of possibly the most sinister and cutthroat members of society.

The youth of today are recruited and socialised into drug gang subculture at younger and younger ages through the social operation and cultural legitimation in the music industry of the drug economies 'illegitimate opportunity structures', because very little exists in terms of truly achievable social mobility for these individuals; to make something of their lives, so the levelling up in the ranks of the drug economy becomes their only realistic and achievable life goal. The true extent of the social problem of drug abuse, drug related crime and drug addiction increases with every successive generation, with new drugs and a lack of an adaptive model of social policy coming out of the think tanks beyond the draconian attitudes that are still prevalent in our social thinking and policy making fifty years after the Misuse of Drugs Act came into effect.

The unknown psychopharmacological effects, addictive natures and 'lifeworld' realities of new legal highs need to be compensated for by groundbreaking and revolutionary policy, such as implemented in 2017 in Edinburgh. Where those suffering from heroin addiction were adequately catered for and admitted to hospitals to be healed of their addiction, instead of convicted of a crime and forced into a prison system to inevitably become socialised into a life of a career criminal.

The problem we face in society today is mirrored by the social problems of the Alcohol prohibition era in the United States of America during the early 19th century. With alcohol use and addiction forced underground, the 'illegitimate opportunity structures' that it created, fueled the mafia and street gang culture of the early 19th century until Alcohol's legalisation; then the problem effectively ceased to be reported in the mass-media. The globalisation of drug taking and the million-dollar drug industry is fuelling the destruction of what we consider the ideals, norms and values of our society and our way of life, even if we don't see it happening because its nature is insidious, underground and subversively subcultural.

Not only this but the current three-tier system of class (a), (b) and class (c) makes very little if no sense, it seems too arbitrary and over-simplistic to be effective at preventing drug abuse. A system in which drugs are placed into a category following no system of true risk analysis. A classification system following no set criteria in which there is no true basis for a reason why each drug is placed in any particular category and with penalties that defy the scale of the harm done to society.

The order of drug risk categorisation needs to be changed and new drug law social policy drafted if we are to protect and guide the future generations to not become abusers of drugs, but instead if they do choose so, to use drugs with responsibly and with an open, informed discerning mind as to the consequences and dangers of recreational drug use. Not an opinionated and easily persuaded closed mind which is dominated by cultural misinformation, mass-media hype and overbearing peer pressure.

In the relatively recent years of its effective implementation in Scotland, where the decriminalisation of Heroin and the providing of accessible places where heavy heroin users could inject their drugs safely, has prevented many drug deaths, prevented the spread of aids and intravenous blood borne virus transmission and caused a 95% drop in drug related crime. As the case study shows this is the best way of preventing the risks involved in drug abuse and shows some of the effectiveness of liberal attitudes and open-minded thinking that is necessary to guide the future of our society.

Using Goode & Ben Yehuda's updated research methodology to the effective study of 'moral panic' emergence, including the original model from Stanley Cohen's Folk Devil's & Moral Panics from the 1960's. I shall analyse how the mass media sensationalization and demonisation of the 'legal high' Novel Substances Act (2016) targets the cultural underclass the socially excluded so that drug taking is to be seen as an outrageous act of scum and villainy in an 'it's them versus us' bilateral stratification of socialised mass-media enculturated opinion and public body decision making socio-political influence.

Where stigmatising labels are permanently affixed and 'self-fulfilling prophecies' subsequently created and people's tangents of life consequently become more and more negative becoming victims of drug abuse, as current drug culture adopts damaging and destructive labels in the negative enforcing of failing drug policy and laws. A sociocultural stagnation where drug dealing gangs are through the mass media music industry portrayed as the powerful socially mobile idols and heroes of the 'drugs war' and the 'illegitimate opportunity structures' through which drug users and victims of excessive drug use begin to self identify as underclass 'waste-man' scum, incapable of living a normal life, succeeding in their aspirations or often even making rational decisions by themselves without the aid of illegal drugs.

These 'illegitimate opportunity structures' exist within society through the monetary incentives offered by the black market economy; that present to the disadvantaged, disempowered and the insecure alternative potential methods of operating in society which offer a way to provide the individual a way of achieving what they believe through the mass media culture industry they through the actualisation of the money and power driven aspiration believe they have always wanted in life. That through the actualisation of their aspirations to the next degree of grandeur, power and notoriety through the globalised illegal drug trade black market economy 'illegitimate opportunity structures' operating within underground society believe they can now achieve. Opportunity perceived where the gains are high (such as in crack cocaine) and risks are less than the countermeasures they can deploy for the achievement of the individuals assumed potential gains. This is when persuaded individuals take up the opportunity to become street drug dealers and become a part of the globalised 'gang culture' of the international black market drug economy.

This for many years through the pushing of drug use underground is how drug use and violent gang related drug crime is growing and it is predominently created by the current drug laws and mass-media driven aspirations for financial success and self actualisation in an otherwise academically restricted mainstream culture of widespread social exclusion and restricted upwards mobility pushing the individual ideals of most people further out of reach. Through the 'blanket ban' of recreational drugs and the irresponsible harmful and damaging opinions driving the current drug policies punitive illegality based categorisation of recreational drugs, the problem still worsens.

With a lack of real foresight towards effective drug abuse rehabilitation and responsible social countermeasures for the socially excluded and those on the fringe of society, inclusive to the increasingly harsh punishments for simple recreational drug use and possession, fueled by a mass media manipulated false state of policy influencing socio-cultural consensus, the situation seems to be in deadlock against the users themselves. A situation whereby instead of rehabilitating drug users we send them to prison where they become socialised into lifechoices making them new career criminals to be further exploited. You end up going to prison for a drug use or possession crime and then a few years later socialised with the most dangerous 1% of society you come out of prison initiated into gang culture able to kill a man with your bare hands.

This creates within the parsonian organic functioning of hegemonic society, and the psychology of the individual drug user, an emotional and intellectual conceptualisation determining an introspective feedback loop of causation. Individually manifest as 'self fulfilling prophecies' where labels are acquired and applied by the individual to themselves creating the life-tangent altering effects of a 'self-fulfilling prophecy' through the individuals' choice of drug use and involvement in mass media fueled drug culture. This in turn is leading to the operation of the fundamental mechanisms of action of the whole system of causation that the media industry, politicians and social commentators have created yet are supposed to protect us from: the stigma of drug abuse.

The only way to break the chains of this self-destructive system is to change the social policies which determine the current drug laws in order to positively influence and change the nature of legitimate experimentation and subsequent dynamics of drug use culture, changing the dynamics of drug rehabilitation for the utilitarian greater good. In order to do this and shed light on a future path towards positive and progressive cultural, individual and collective social destiny I shall be investigating the Novel Substances Act (2016) 'legal highs blanket ban' as an example of the 'war on drugs' covert reporting agenda is the deliberate instigation of a mass media moral panic. One designed to exasperate the social policy influencing effects of culturally ignorant and individually damaging sentimental beliefs, opinions and labels in the creation of self-fulfilling prophecies that are applied to recreational drug users to demonise and criminalise their behaviours and prevent effective social policy implementation and liberal minded cultural change.

It is the ideological, cultural and philosophical intention of this pioneering piece of research work to consider the fundamental mechanisms of action and angles of causation which determine how mass media reports control and dominate the social attitudes, cultural opinions and political agendas of society. It's final conclusion will set out a rational and logical solution to the social problem of drug abuse than the quick fix legislation of the 1970's half a century ago; this speculative sociocultural philosophy for future drug policy will primarily consider the fundamental factors of:

A) The risk to health, danger and toxicity of the drug considered, along with the potentiality and proximity of the associated dangers and risks of its consumption.

B) The addictiveness as in the strength of the psychological and physiological effects of the drug and onset of the individual's addiction to it.

C) The factor of the individuals personal tolerance/intolerance to a recreational psychoactive substance and technological innovations that can be deployed in ways of the incorporation of this factor and mediation of the drugs harmful or damaging effects.

D) The factor of the purity/impurity of the psychoactive substance consumed, for the risks to be accurately considered and the extent to which the standardisation of the quality of the drug can be legitimately introduced and maintained in order to reduce risks to the drug user.

E) The level of education and informed awareness of the inherent risks involved in drug use to which a person can be made aware as a preventive measure to reduce the social extent of the negative consequences of recreational drug use.

Informed individuals are therefore more enabled to make wiser and more intelligent choices and competent risk reducing decisions towards illicit drug use than are individuals blinded by ignorance, peer pressure or consensus swaying emotive and manipulative sensationalism in the cultural mass media.

To conclude this introductory section our social life tangents are determined by the causations of 'self-fulfilling prophecies' which have created a label we have internalised and now believe. A label acquired from a perceived authority making them an individual drug dealer or a drug user and individuals then sculpt their self-concept and self-image. In the process of living up to those applied labels to become the oppressive drug dealers, looking for victims to make examples of to secure their next social mobility jump, or the insecure victims of drug abuse who tolerate the scarcity of social mobility and opportunity outside of the illegitimate opportunity structures resigning to a life of superficial drug induced satisfaction and pleasure.

This piece of social sciences research will specifically look at how the 'War on Drugs' can be viewed as a 'Moral Panic' and continues operation in shaping our current social attitudes and political opinions around drug crime which influence future social policy decisions. Considering throughout the covert and subtle ways that the currently operating 'Illegitimate Opportunity Structures' through the conditioning and socialisation of the young and insecure in our society into their subcultural gang culture ranks to either become new dominating career criminals or subordinated drug user is systemic of the self induced social crisis of drug use.

Theoretical Background:

The conceptual origin of the most fundamental sociological term used in the formulation of this research piece, through the words of the individual person who coined the phrase; 'moral panic' was Stanley Cohen. In his breakthrough piece of research into the sociology of deviance and it's reporting in the mass media, Cohen's book, Folk Devil's & Moral Panics defines the concept of a media defined 'folk devil' or labelled deviant of a 'moral panic' is to be most fundamentally considered through a sociological lens when a:

"Condition, episode, person or group of persons emerges to become defined as a threat to societal values and interests"
-Cohen, S. (1972)

A social issue or problem is of being of the fundamental nature of a perceived threat to society, it can be said that a mass media highlighted deviant is a specific targeted individual whose individual behaviours, social decisions or cultural choices is in its most basic essence one which impinges upon, contradicts or undermines the cultural traditions social values, political interests or the general consensus of collectively held beliefs and opinions that a community or society is commonly understood by the overwhelming majority to collectively share.

To operationalize this definition of deviance and put it another more simple way, it is anything which can be defined as a perceived sociocultural entity or object which operates and exists outside the boundaries of the commonly accepted socio-cultural definitions of the shared similarity of meaning and experience. As such of the generalised common social actor, within society whose accepted frames of reference and general interpretive comprehension of a universally accepted and shared societal and cultural dynamics of general individual understanding cannot comprehend.

The social and cultural definitions of the specific psychological or behavioural nature of an individual's deviance in their social interactions, symbolic cultural stylistic differences, and

15

nonlinearity to the traditionally accepted cultural norms. Which can be specifically labelled as significantly deviant as the individuals and groups, through definitive identifiable differences of the symbolic stylistic individuation of their personal identity, are unanimously and uniquely associated with specific outlier subcultural meanings.

A deviant individual is a person whose stylistic symbols of cultural significance and social interaction are thus through the process of a moral panic labelled as a deviation from the fundamental conceptually accepted definitions of normality. Done so through the oversimplification of common understandings further culturally ingrained in the minds of individuals within our society through being commented upon in the mass-media, whereby the reactive levels of emotivity contained within our conceptual definitions are fundamentally elevated to create a false consensus of hegemonic coercion.

This emotive elevation is further reinforced through the social commentaries of public officials and cultural representatives, who aim to cease such perceived deviant activities or behaviours through instilling within us a general sense of consensus in the form of a shared sentiment of collective opinion; through controlling of the flow of political influence and cultural thought through the social apparatus of the mass media. As such the opinions of the general population in the course of the progressive stages of the moral panic through these spokespeople exerting their capacities of their positions of authority and power within their individual circles of social association and personal political influence which they operate within are essentially the gatekeepers of the social decision making process. According to the work of Stanley Cohen, there are five main stages to the appearance, development and cessation of a moral panic; these are:

1. A particular deviant behaviour or group of individuals is defined as a threat to our society, to our safety and to our individual personal interests.

2. The perceived deviant threat is amplified by the mass media over-reporting, exemplified through the use of sensationalising simplistic rhetoric.

3. Reactive social anxieties are further heightened through symbolically manipulative emotivity in the reporting styles and through pictorial exaggerations in the representation of the social issue.

4. Official gatekeepers of cultural opinion and respected social experts denounce the labelled deviance and pronounce official diagnoses and voice reactionary opinionated responses to the public in order to limit and lessen the social and cultural effects of the perceived threat.

5. The social conditions determining the label of deviance undergoes radical and significant change through the deviant presence submerging through social policy implementation, deteriorating as a result. Or the deviant threat becomes culturally integrated into socially accepted definitions of normality and becomes inclusively visible in everyday life.

This is Cohen's basic groundwork of the five fundamental stages of a moral panic, i now incorporate the follow up academic work of the social theorists of deviance and mass-media research Erich Goode and Nachman Ben-Yehuda's work in their book; Moral Panics: The Social Construction of Deviance (2009). In this work they highlight the specific fundamental mechanisms of action which effectively perpetuate the dynamics of causation involved in, functional origins of and the final end state of the termination of a 'moral panic'. This is known within the field as the 'attributional model' and defines a moral panics ontological nature as a sociocultural entity with the fundamental nature of its operation as being of one of the three following mutually non-exclusive theoretical perspectives and paradigms of rational causation and socio-scientific understanding.

1) The first potential explanation of how a 'moral panic' develops and comes to exist is the 'grassroot operation' analysis. Here we see a belief that a 'moral panic' operates primarily and most fundamentally at the grassroots level, where the manifestation of the sociocultural phenomena is resultant of the real and genuine cultural reaction to the symbolic emotional nature of the intellectual fixations produced through the social anxieties at work through the 'moral panic' becoming actual and into being. They exist as a product of the reactionary individual cultural reflexes to the symbolic realities of the perceived social threats associated with the identification, signification and experience of the socially labelled and culturally defined entities of social and cultural deviance.

2) The second of these three definitive models of explanation is known as 'elite engineering theory'. This perspective holds that 'moral panics' are intentionally created in a direct attempt by the ruling socio-economic elite, to control the future and destiny of our society, through systematic manipulation of the mass-media in order to instigate a superficial and false yet socially believed as true symbolic perception of the prevalent and dominant cultural consensus of stable opinion and shared cultural meaning. A 'moral panic' is the instigation of an effective emotionally constituted cultural counterbalance to the symbolic doubt raised by the fundamental questioning of the assumed sociocultural legitimation of normality, the bedrock upon which the economic owners elitist power and 'lifeworld' social order is effectively created and maintained. The manifestation of all cultural or social deviations from the collectively accepted definitions of our societies ideological concepts of normality, is perceived by the economic ruling elite as a fundamental and insidious threat to societies fragile state of current social order and stability and is seen as a direct challenge to the hierarchical legitimation of their economic, social and political power and dominant elitist ideology of control. Through manipulating prevalent public sentiment and cultural and political opinions through the influence of the mass media in the form of sensationalist over-reporting and excessive repetition in news reporting and story headlines, through the inherent

over-emotivity in the reporting styles of the individuals involved, it reinforces a sense of collective social and cultural order and consensus and also diverts attention away from other articles which could be considered more newsworthy. News articles which undermine, sideline and marginalise other more significant reports are a key feature in a 'moral panic' and through this covert reporting methodology at work demonstrates the socio-political and economically enabled elitism that owns and operates the cultural and political institutions, which are acutely and profoundly incompetent in their attempts to effectively deal with, cope and solve the many different societal problems and dominant international crises that dominate the human condition currently in existence.

3) The third potential reason for as to why moral panics occur is known as 'interest group theory', which operate due to differences of intellectual understanding, emotional constitution and personal taste which operate in the individual dissemination and choice of news media sources. The specific targeting and consequent influences upon our beliefs, attitudes and opinions is different for all members of society. The hierarchical stratification of society through employment in the job market is according to our individual level of actualised educational potential, developed through the learning of a concept dependant intellectual paradigm of information interpretation and rationalisation. This is developed throughout the individual life-course and initiated through academic study, engendering consequent causations of social association and shared sub-culturally significant shared symbolic meanings. The cultural dissemination of analytic and synthetic information about current affairs and popular opinion through tabloid news literature, because of the nature of individual differences and personal preferences needs to be sufficiently tailored to suit the different cultural requirements and educational demands of the newspaper consuming discerning reader. Therefore due to the way in which the separate hierarchically aligned social strata can be generalised in nature through educational achievement and consequent employment roles and associated social class alignments, specifically middle-class and

working-class social groups of readers have necessarily different requirements and demands upon the literature they seek and consume. For each social strata of general class association is also differently targeted by the respective different newspapers according to the specific interests and demands of the reader. To specify this targeting, of these groups, the working-class tend to have less complex informational demands and discursive requirements of their chosen news sources, and have a higher degree of emotional receptivity and reactive moral sensitivity than the academically developed and intellectually enabled emotional sublimation of middle-class readers. Therefore the natural differences of representative opinionation and emotional sensibility integral to the fundamental nature of the instrumental reasoning deployed by different newspaper publications in order to gain the favour of readers and further their own private economic interests and political agendas, fits well with the inherent functional dynamics of causation innate to manifestation and maintenance of an active 'moral panic' in its fullest entirety. Specific symptoms of a 'moral panic' such as the increase in emotional charge in the conceptual signification to an unnecessary high level of over-emotivity in the report style of the topics involved and the presentation of the article concerned, as well as the fundamentally misleading oversimplification of rhetorical terms with a tendency towards stereotype and ridicule in its semantic expression; is evidence of the methodological deployment of instrumental reasoning in the pursuit of financial objectives of a inherently capitalist ideology. A further point must also be made in retrospect of stating these three different theoretical perspectives, that a situational parallelism of dynamic causation exists between the explanation of the perspectives of both the Elite Engineering Theory and Interest Group Theory , which could represent a further correspondence of fundamental factors as a cause of concern.

This alignment of potentially hazardous socio-cultural situation and the dynamics of both naturally occurring disseminative and potentially synthetically instigated causation within the operation of economic and political ideologies within the inside of the social institution of the mass-media could produce a social state of mass cultural coercion of thoughts, beliefs and opinions. Should these processes and dynamics at work in mass media consumption be exploited through the social and political influence of the economic elite for their own covert ideological goal driven ends, their individual personal desires or for the collective gain of their inherent social strata of subcultural association and the potential for a covert secret agenda could be instigated against the people to control the creation of false consensus.

It can be said that the mass media institutions are fundamental in triggering the early stages of a moral panic and in producing symbolically coded images and buzz word conceptual definitions of societal and cultural significance regarding deviance. Done through manipulation of public thought with the striking and profound definition of perceived yet abstract social threats into a visual representation as a pictorial control form. The symbolic interactionist school of thought would state these social control forms take the shape of:

1) The distortion and exaggeration of what those labelled as deviant did or said in the form of what is initially reported and represented.

2) The further prediction of social discord and dire consequences for all citizens, should society and societies members fail to take heed and act upon the culturally engendering recommendations of the highly emotive news reports.

3) The characteristic symbolisation of a specific new forms of deviance in the symbolic representation of a particular person, group, buzz-word, object or perceived threat in the mainstream news reporting of the mass media.

Eventually through these reporting processes and dynamics we see moral entrepreneurs, social influencers, official representatives and respected cultural spokespeople targeting the deviant individuals, groups and their definitively distinct labelled behaviours as a form of moral social control, in order to preserve the socially perceived traditional definitions of accepted cultural normality. This means involving and mobilising the institutional powers, the police, county courts and legal partitions in order to combat the reality of the instilled fear and panic as a response to the perceived deviant threat in order to reinforce objective social control and legitimate public opinion.

The war on drugs officially began in 1971 with the then President Richard Nixon declaring the social problem of drug abuse as 'public enemy number one'. Since then millions of dollars have been invested every year to try to rid society of its illegal drug availability, to a total tax expenditure of more than one trillion dollars. More than half a century later we are still fighting the 'war on drugs' during which time drug use and drug abuse has escalated further, becoming a more prevalent and prominent social issue than in the decades since the war began. It appears to many people concerned that the 'war on drugs' has not delivered on its promise and that something new is desperately needed to replace the failed policy and Ideology; which can effectively deliver humanity from the darkness of its drug addiction.

"Making drugs more available will make it harder to keep our communities healthier and safe"

-President Richard Nixon (1971)

Since this statement half a century ago in more recent years (2011) the official body the global commission on drug policy has been quoted as stating on the record: 'the global war on drugs has failed.'.

There are many factors involved, but perhaps the main reason why the 'war on drugs' has failed to protect us from the consequences of drug use and abuse is because of its insidious underground cultural nature. The structures and means through which the drug dealing gang orientated subculture in the modern day which is reinforced by the mass media and the symbolic representations of wealth and power in the mainstream music and images which catch the keen interest of youthful eyes are dominant in the process of its perpetuation.

Due to the potential for drug users and dealers to be recruited from any walk of life and from a relatively young age, regardless of their original social demographic, or economic status, we see constant repeated cycles of self-perpetuating social deprivation and inequality. Add to this the monetary incentive from drug sales, especially with high risk drugs like methamphetamine or crack cocaine, where the amount of potential profit eclipses the experienced economic deprivation of the underclasses and we see that the problem multiplies in its scale exponentially.

The highest level of operation in the drugs dealing system is ultimately that of the internationally globalised illegal import and export trade routes of the black market economy. Through links to terrorism and the inherent corruption of oppressive political regimes, who maximise their control over domestic challengers to their power base so compromises the global integrity of the socioeconomic stability of the planet; yet another of capitalisms negative side effects within the macrocosmic system the operation of 'illegitimate opportunity structures' of the black market economy given their international totality of true causation.

The origin of the term 'illegitimate opportunity structure' lies within the work of the criminologists and sociological theorists of youth, deviance and subculture; Richard Cloward and Lloyd Ohlin. In their book Delinquency and Opportunity: A Theory of Delinquent Gangs (1960), it states within its pages that deviant subcultural organisations represent for the socially disadvantaged and economically challenged members of society, in particular the underclasses and youths who are caught in the grip of downward social mobility, a cross-stratification parallel of individual opportunity and success, matching the idealised perceptions of personal success and social actualisation percieved in the aspirational roles that are represented in mainstream culture.

Hence the 'illegitimate opportunity structures' operating within society at the underground level, offer individuals, where the perceived gain is more significant than the potential risks, the potential to invest time, money and resources, to become upwardly socially mobile. This is done through exploiting the presented opportunities they encounter naturally and create themselves, as they desire, within the boundaries and scope of their 'lifeworld' situation; the fundamental reason why drug crime occurs, and has become such a prevalent public and social issue.

A.K. Cohen (1955) presents a perspective associating educational youth delinquency and working-class economic deprivation, as a response to a perceived lack of social mobility and opportunity in inner city areas. With the potential of organised crime as a way to succeed, following the stifling of educational potential and drop out from the ordinary job market, subcultural social structures come to exist which promote achievement through the cultural agency of the illicit drug economy.

The theory of W. Miller in (1958) and (1959) describes the formation of deviant social associations, which essentially define the nature of the gang subculture creation as a 'way of life.' Once an individual has become involved with and socialised into, through the the rite of initiation, into operational gang deviance. It can be very hard to disengage from the subcultural behaviours, personal ties and shared ontological similarities between the gang members, to formally leave the group and the inherently confining empathetic, social and cultural bonding.

There are supporting theoretical ideas from F.T. Thrasher (1927), that subcultural groups are 'originally formed spontaneously and then integrated through conflict'. The socially conditioning reinforcement of daily activities into a 'way of life' involves 'meeting face-to-face, milling, movement through space as a unit, conflict and planning'. Also included along similar lines are the ideas of E.F. Fraser (1957) about the social disorganisation of gangs and the creation of an underclass, which has also been also been discussed in Garfoot, A.P. (2010) as a potential source of revolutionary cultural agency and social change.

R.L Moreland and J.M. Levine in (1982) discuss how individuals become socialised into subcultural groups through their personal associations. In their work they discuss five main stages to group socialisation and subcultural membership:

1) Investigation: This is where the subcultural group and socialisation into it meets personal needs of the individual. Such as consistency of belief and what the social group's culture represents

in its true nature as it incorporates the value of a new member into its subcultural ways and social associations. This is done through the phase known as reconnaissance and recruitment where we see a combination of push and pull factors bringing an individual into a subculture through the mutual operation of both of these social processes.

2) Socialisation: As in the process of socialisation itself, where the individual accepts the norms, values, perceived ideals and perspectives of the subcultural group; a process known as assimilation. As a response the group adapts its structure of social associations to incorporate it's new members' needs, in order to grow in size and increase its power and influence.

3) Maintenance: This is where the individual members of a group negotiate the social expectations of each other, called role negotiation; the failure of an individual to meet their expectations is called divergence. The sub-culturally accepted normal clothing styles and the previous attitudes and perspectives of the groups prior members are incorporated according to the aspirations and beliefs of the new members.

4) Resocialization: Where divergent members operating on the fringe of the group become full members again, through convergence, or the way in which a group member exposes their difference of opinion and are expelled and made to leave the group. Through divergent beliefs compromising the integrity of the subcultural group, into which the individual has attempted to become socialised, members may enforce their collective opinions and social influence over them.

5) Remembrance: Is where an individual or a group shares memories of having once been a part of subculture. This becomes a part of the individual's life ontology as an ex-member and also becomes a part of the social and cultural tradition of the group; as it transitions from its prior into its new form.

The social scientist Howard Becker was the symbolic interactionist who devised the original formulation of 'labelling theory' in his groundbreaking piece of social psychology Outsiders: Studies In The Sociology Of Deviance (1963). He investigates how people adopt and incorporate authority ascribed labels from others who are perceived as having legitimate power over them into their 'self image' concept. He defines the symbolic processes and subconscious rules of the social dynamics of interpersonal group interaction, where behavioural change through conceptual conditioning is effected through the alteration and modification to in individuals use of 'self image' conceptualisation.

The instigation of new deviant social attitudes and behaviour patterns in the individual's manifest ways of acting are developed and reinforced through the subconscious object intentionality of the labelling process, which affects every part of an individual's thoughts and mental development. Through the personal objectification and internalisation of external socially created subjective definitions we create, maintain and propagate the attitudes and behaviours and beliefs we encounter in our social associations and personal experiences.

Labelling theory, the symbolic interactionist theory of the nature of the propagation and spread of deviant behaviour, is where a negative or a positive label applied by a dominant individual is internalised and believed as true by a subordinate individual. The label is applied to the self image of the subordinate and the individual's unique characteristic attitude, nature, lifestyle and behaviour. It is transmitted subconsciously through the focus of intentionally of the projected thoughts or beliefs of a person in a perceived position of accepted authority to a person assumed subordinate through their social interactions.

The process of the internalisation of labels, is where through modification made to self image, an individual lives up to a label ascribed by another, in an imbalance of self belief and personal power. The subordinated individual undergoes an identity shift, as new labels are incorporated into their self identity, so that their self-image and self-concept; their manifest self changes in its fundamental nature.

The feedback loop which operates at the level of the social will, between social authority figures and the individual is where the labelling of deviance occurs, the personal exemplification of action through the internalisation of these labels. The modification to externalised behaviour through this feedback loop, of conditioning through introspection and socialisation, are the result of the individual being influenced at the level of the subconscious will is how the feedback loop is formed.

Tattenbaum (1938) describes the primary process of subcultural growth in society as 'tagging', whereby an individual loses sight of their previous identity and adopts new subcultural and divergent labels and roles. These are not necessarily or essentially deviant in nature as these labels are a part of the greater socio-cultural representation of individual definition and belief. In the initial creation of subcultural growth however, superficial definitions and beliefs are adopted, yet are still to be fully internalised and integrated into the newly forming identity the individual is assuming, which eventually solidifies and becomes their accepted perception of their personal identity and definition of social normality.

Robert K Merton in his work studying the ontological determination of an individual's progressive life-course, through the altering nature of interaction with social structures, institutions and authority looks at how previous social situations and psychological factors play out to create future social situations and grounding psychological dispositions. Based upon the theoretical definitions of 'labelling theory' (1996 ed.), he looks at how positive and negative beliefs determine the creation of future life situations, through the socio-temporal causation of their manifest self image and self concept orientation through the progressive creation of the term he coins as a 'self fulfilling prophecy'.

We internalise socially learnt labels and individualise them through the frame of reference of our cultural identity, through the subconscious processes of our thought patterns through the dynamics of the conditioning process of socialisation. These identities we create affect our individual personal choices and the development of our life chances and potentials, effecting through them our projected free will in the present moment into our social interactions, future life situations and the outcome of our life course.

Experimental Methodology:

This research piece will primarily consist of a quantitatively inclusive analysis formed of a computed emotivity value & statistical graph and histogram of progression data comparison. This emotivity ratio is composed of an emotional word count for each article, divided by the number of non-emotive words in the same article. The broadcast News Reports are from BBC News in the years (2012-2016).

The Report Emotivity Data table has been converted into further demographic representations of a comparative cross-section of the analytical time window. A qualitative perspective and quantitative methodology of critical focus analysis which shall include frequently used emotionally charged descriptive content, buzzwords, over emotive signification, counterintuitive statements and intentional over and under reporting will be deployed in this study.

Descriptive phrasing such as 'crazed drug addicts' or 'zombie spice heads' will be included in the results as an example of a possible covert agenda operating within the reports, representative of instigating bias at least as much as an individual intersubjective reporting style. I will also look for broad similarities between the television broadcasts of the different emergent reporting inquiry pattern engineering which has been used to maximum effect, to be used as evidence of this ideologically determined polemic operating between personal intersubjectivism, and operationalised elitism.

Similar reporting techniques will produce a different ratio baseline for the time window, and can be viewed as evidence of an intentionally manipulative elitist methodology at work, within the consensus influencing effects of the mass media in society. These reporting styles I will look for as evidence of what Goode and Ben Yehuda's work would determine to be a covert elitist agenda at work, within the broad time period cross-section of the broadcast media analysis.

This piece of research will try to capture evidence of the five main characteristics of Stanley Cohen and Goode & Ben Yehuda's research work. These previously highlighted factors for analysis are; (a) concern, (b) hostility, (c) consensus, (d) disproportionality and finally (e) volatility. In the statistical analysis I shall deploy graphically, to produce appropriate visual representation, a demonstration of the linear statistical progression of the moral panic through quantitative visualised expression of the inherent causation to the system of numerical qualification; conceptual triangulation will reinforce this evidential claim and theoretical position I am taking.

The key statistical formulation to achieve this objective is the 'report emotivity ratio' which will be reinforced by the triangulation methods of contextual qualitative data, to be represented in the results along together; for support coordinating the further conclusions I draw. The outcome of this process will be to accurately define the reports in the forthcoming results and analysis section to see if there are any tendencies represented in the overall analysis and any clear cut indications of emotional bias of a personal, ideological, covert manipulation or a significant statistical pattern otherwise in the results data of the research.

The graphical representation of contextual content and statistical analysis over the time frame of the study, will enable further objectivity and support or occlude and compromise, the theoretical claims of the previous sociological research by said social scientists, in the relevant subject areas and if successful will provide a sound basis for further examination of such research work in the area in the future.

In order to complete this research task successfully I have highlighted both quantitatively and qualitatively the fundamental distinctions between reports highlighted in the research synthesis of Stanley Cohen, and Goode and Ben Yehuda's five main phases that signify the evidence of a moral panic in its various operational stages in the British Broadcasting Company mass media news reports during the critical time window of the analysis. The five main significantly distinct stages of the moral panic I am looking for are:

1) Concern- Initial emotive reporting of a 'them versus us' attitude, all moral panics are exemplified by a heightened consensus instigating level of emotional response in the first reports and

personal concern is guided to a perceived but essentially fabricated objectification, of a newly formed or discovered personal, social or cultural threat.

2) Hostility- The target deviant individuals, group or social behaviour consisting of recreational legal high drug use and drug users are designated as a distinct and immediate enemy or threat to the safety and moral integrity of greater society. This consists of a continued 'them versus us' reporting attitude of exaggerated social concern and negative emotional representation of the targeted individuals; relative to the sociopolitical agendas and reporting styles innate of the mass media news reports.

3) Consensus- Social entrepreneurs, moral commentators, policy decision makers and politicians become publicly focused on and vocal in designating the target group of recreational psychoactive drug users as a significant and dangerous threat to society. Whilst trying to undermine the group integrity and cultural revolutionary potential of the targeted individuals and group. Through a general attempt at making the public believe that through labelling the socially excluded target group of drug use and users as a threat, but weak, deviant and socially disorganised; whereas the general public are strong, morally justified and socioculturally coherent.

4) Disproportionality- This is where social concern over the danger and negative social consequences of the excluded and targeted deviant behaviour labelled under the buzzword 'legal high' outweighs and is an exaggeration of the genuine risk of harm that such use poses to concerned members of the general public. These news reports of concern are given precedence over other more newsworthy headline articles representing greater threats to social harmony and greater risks to personal safety and security such as war, invasion, famine, death, murder or genocide. Anything which can be considered a more prevalent and important social issue is sidelined to give recreational legal high consumption and behaviours pinnacle reporting headline space.

5) Volatility- The final culminating stage of the moral panic, volatility, is represented through new laws and social policy being introduced to counteract the perceived social threat, in this case through the introduction of the (2016) 'legal high' Psychoactive Substances Act. This is when public interest wanes over recreational drug use, as other news stories of more important content take precedence over the behaviours of the targeted deviant individuals and the moral panic, it seems, is to have ended as a new narrative begins within the mass media news representation and reports.

Results Analysis:

This is my primarily qualitative analysis of the mass media reports of the BBC for the 'legal high' Novel Psychoactive Substances 'moral panic' 2012-2016.

Initially there was one report made in (2012), six reports made in (2013) two reports made in (2014) four reports made in (2015) and six reports made in (2016) when the Novel Substances Act or 'blanket ban' was passed and came into effect, ending the moral panic.

Of the (2013) and (2012) reports, featured are the comments from the officials of several important public bodies. Official comments were made by people from: The Home Office, United Nations, the European Commissioner for Home Affairs, The Crime Prevention Minister and the Director of Public Health alone in (2014). The United Nations Office on Drugs also at least at one point offered official comment also.

In (2015) the news report comments focused particularly around the city of Lincoln and around medical professionals. In the (2016) build up to the introduction of the Novel Substances Act 'blanket ban' all of the media reports featured specifically from mental health illness sufferers uses of drugs or grieving parents.

This is except for the period of time after the Novel Substances Act (2016) blanket ban came into force in which case the commentators were officials such as the Deputy Director for London Ambulance Service and quoted official Police reports and comments on arrests and seizures after the Novel Substances Act came into effect.

The (2013) reports are mainly based around mephedrone which was a previously non-illicit 'legal high' which became outlawed in (2012) leading on into the 'threat' of new novel psychoactive legal highs towards the end of (2013) after the mephedrone legal high moral panic ended with tough new legislation and enforcement measures for supply and possession coming into effect.

The year of (2014) saw only two BBC reports about novel psychoactive substances, both of which are non significant in their emotivity. In (2015) reports were not particularly emotive until the point when the 'blanket ban' became speculated in the political arena. This is when the most emotive report appeared of a grieving mother followed by the emotive reporting of a further three reports in the space of two months as opposed to 2015 during the warming phase to where four reports covered the entire year.

The highest amount of over-reporting was in (2016) of the months April to May, flooding the mass media with emotional stories of bereaved families and recovering drug addicts in the weeks prior to the point at which the Novel Substances Act (2016) came into effect outlawing all 'legal highs'.

The second most of the most prominently defined areas of over-reporting would have been in (2013) concerning the once 'legal high' mephedrone before the legislative end to its recreational reign as a designer party drug. The report also follows the progression of the legal high novelty trend and its extension into the future as becoming a further threat to society, the danger and threat to society of further legal high designer drug proliferation. All reports of which were given headline space were between March and September of that year, with three reports all appearing in June.

The most emotive report was made in April (2016), a month before Novel Substances Act (2016) 'blanket ban' came into effect. It featured 32 emotive words for the total of 420 words in the released report. The least emotive report was made in January of (2015) the previous year, which featured 19 emotive words for a total of 940 non-emotive words.

The least emotive phase of reporting would have been from January 2nd (2015) to December the 2nd (2015) featuring the 17th 19th and 20th least emotive reports that have been studied in this piece of research.

There is prominent over emotivity in reporting at the very beginning of the moral panic study period of analysis from the date of the 25th of April (2012) to the 7th of the March (2013) in which there were 3 reports; the 3rd, 2nd and 5th most emotive reports, presumably to strike fear into the heart of the general public and instil consensus in the decision making political body.

The first phase of over reporting in (2013) ends with official comments from: The Director of Public Health, The Crime

Prevention Minister, The United Nations, The Home Office Minister and The European Commission For Home Affairs.

The second phase of over reporting does not mention any particular officials who commented who are of particular public stature, or notably important, but to reinforce the message they try to hit home that drugs are dangerous and only have inherently evil or just plain bad consequences for all individuals concerned or involved in their use.

This is as all the reports tend to include comments from grieving mothers or people who suffer the negative side of drug addictions, who have only just escaped their drug addiction in order to send to the public a message of heroic sentimental consensus towards the introduction of the Novel Substances Act (2016) and against any controversy, comment or opinion contrary within the general public body against such a political notion.

The BBC report of the 13th of May (2016) features the most qualitatively emotional nature of any of the reports, describing the death of two brothers 'fighting legal highs addiction' who had both lived together and lost their lives, including the embittered desperation of their grieving mother as the focal point of the television article. What the report also includes almost as a footnote is that both brothers had been intravenously injecting heroin addicts for many years since their early teens, perhaps a more prevalent factor upon the brothers short lived life spans as this happens to be the most extreme and damaging form of drug use and addition; which was given secondary status to the use of 'spice' and it's psychological effects of psychosis.

Practically every report made by the BBC featured specifically the social and individual harms to health that legal highs do. In particular the unknown nature of the exact specific harm many 'legal highs' cause, due to their unknown mechanisms of action and pharmacological nature, creates limitations as to what paramedics and doctors can effectively do to help treat the underlying cause of the manifest symptoms of an overdose, without causing more harm or being ineffective.

Also mentioned were foreign countries of production and origin such as the Far East Asia and India, which were specifically named for housing numerous 'breaking bad style' laboratories producing these novel substances for sale online.

Two reports as such were both covering Lincoln City Council's stance on novel substances, recreational legal high use having had the worst case of arrests and hospitalisation incidents involving the emergency services. Comments not on violence and aggression but on 'general disobedience' were alluded to by the press, but as to what this means can be left to the imagination considering the recreational nature drugs involved.

After the novel substances act (2016) was passed there were only two more news reports made which were archived by the British Broadcasting Company. The first was released the day after the Novel Substances Act (2016) was passed; the other followed three months afterwards. It is at this point where the 'moral panic' can be said to have officially ended through the efficacy of the legislative response to the perception of social deviance leading to the cessation due to the lack of necessity of further news reporting space.

Discussion:

The 'war on drugs' is not simply a war on drugs, but has deeper anti-liberal philosophical roots than that. It is a war on one's choice of recreational consciousness, through the mechanics of enforced pharmaceutical materialist coercion.

It is a war on the choice of one's own person to think in a particular style, or experience a type of thought or perception different to others. A war against our individual personal choices and decisions regarding thought and the freedom of it, through our own unadulterated natural freedom and ability to make choices without others deciding for us.

This is going to be an ideological breakdown, of how the war on drugs controls us at the root core level of causation as a civilisation. How was the instigated way of an elite, to control the consciousness of the planet against its own choosing, against its own knowledge, its best wishes and against its own future enlightenment.

I hold as the starting premise that it is true that our own body is the one object and the only object that we will ever truly own in our life. It is what we are born into at the beginning of our existence and the one thing that we leave when we pass this mortal coil and cease to be alive. So as the Druidic philosophical maxim and Kantian reworking goes, as long as we are not harming anybody else, then who is anybody to say what I should or shouldn't do with my own body or for that matter, to my own body.

Anything which happens in accordance with natural laws, it can be said, is in true alignment with the greater all that is, the inner self of the soul, and our unique higher nature. Therefore it happens in the best ways, for the best reasons, but anything which is forced or unnatural in nature, it can equally be said is in violation with this principle of universal law and therefore against our individual sanctity of choice as an individual and rights as a human being.

The idea that one should be forced to take a drug, for whatever reason, unless it is in accordance with a self or socially protective principle, is just as heinous and against our individual liberty, as it is that one should be forced not to never take a drug, even once, even if we desire so using the fullest capacity of our own choice and full development of our free will. What follows is a detailed breakdown of how a 'moral panic' works at the most fundamental level, in controlling the consciousness and choices of the population of society and of the sociopolitical consensus of the world.

It is said that in the humanities there are theory testing pieces of research and theory building pieces of research, the research testing has been done, now let us build from it. I will now begin with a redefinition of the 'war on drugs' 'moral panic' in light of the research which has been conducted and confirmed in the previous chapters, hence I begin.

As we have noted in this current piece of research, in its first analysis of potentially over-emotive reporting agendas and the detailed findings represented, including comments from many highly official spokespeople, we see how the panic dies out and cessates as soon as new legislation is about to come into force, emotional stories from family members of addicts who lost spouse which become highly publicised to reinforce the emotional sentiment which was triggered in the initial reporting. This can be seen as a style of sensitisation to make sure that an instrumentally reasoning public follows the sentiment of the sensitising elite, in order to control public consensus and reinforce legislative power of an elite political body, Adamson (2014).

The end result is that through following the elitist agendas of the opinion controling mass media, the future and the freedoms of the social body are controlled beyond their knowledge, their means of gaining control over that control, which operates against the peoples better interests, against their future needs and desires as human beings; but most fundamentally against their naturally born with inalienable human rights. This leads to the progressive criminalisation of new drugs as recreational compounds, just for the user to experience an enhanced or less negative state of mind they now become the public enemy of the state and society.

Drug abuse then suddenly becomes a social problem, one which needs controlling, in other words, because the individual chooses to exercise the free choice they have themselves they now apparently need controlling through the criminal justice system. Controlled either finding themselves reprimanded, given a criminal record or sent to prison which in many cases of young individuals is both life-changing and destroying.

The symbolic interactionist perspective of 'labelling theory' applies here as 'self image' altering labels that people in positions of authority; teachers, doctors, judges, police and official representatives give drug users and addict's makes them undermine their self-confidence and begins their future life paths as criminal subordinates. Through internalising these labels in the destruction of their once positive self-image, through the attribution of negative self-image determining concepts, hinders the future life choice aspirations they once had, limiting their ability to actualize the true potential they naturally possessed, through diverting attention away from positive personal traits to negative ones. Manipulated in consciousness through subordinating socialisation in which the individual proceeds to take on deviant or criminal self-image concepts, in which their capacity to self-actualise is truly destroyed, a heinous thing indeed.

The working class individuals who suffer the worst effects of this labelling process, from the early days of the teaching classroom to the days of work in life often incorporate these drug user roles and images into their self-image. They concede by living up to these labels as they become deviant themselves through demoralisation and disempowerment, they are subject to personal changes through the greater socialisation processes at work in the mass media and greater cultural representations of wealth and power considered achievable, P. Willis, (1977).

The disempowerment to self is engendered through the education system, through the mass media, through the criminal justice system and a lack of true social mobility available to the 'down and out', at the bottom of the social hierarchy, where daily there are stark life choices to be made and few pleasures and rewards. Far less than those who stand to gain something from the current social structure, like the upper class elite and their culturally affluent progeny. In our society few can actually gain with the power and wealth polarisation which operates, polarisation which is responsible for the cultural disempowerment of the working classes worldwide and the actual source of true social decay through the mass media in the postmodern era.

The mass media controls us, through the opinions of tabloid newspapers which print these exaggerated news reports, the television news programs which we watch, we take on the opinions of the elite and happily, not knowing the true damage it is doing to our society by accepting the superficial beliefs they proliferate on the grounds that they are from an officially endorsed or popular source. We believe their represented opinions are true because the reports were written by experts and we assume impartial experts at that, without elitist agendas at work and without partial persuasion from their own class bound place in place by their biassed institutions. Our freedom to think and our freedom of choice is slowly being eroded away, taken from us by subtle agendas of the British printing press and mass media corporations of the U.K.

Reports of deviance vary between different media sources, for news reports and general culture alike users are depicted in a negative light and their deviance of drug taking appears to look like the end of society through the encroachment and downfall of our cultural norms and social values. But there is also in mainstream culture itself presented in the mass media subcultural drug use of gang culture on music channels we see the glorifying of violence and promoting opportunistic behaviours, for the sake of effectively achieving personal power, fame, notoriety and glory.

This represents a dichotomous under-evolved form of drug culture as represented in the culture of the mass media, which evokes the question; is drug representation in media due to get worse with young people and gangs becoming more violent and drug abuse and drug addiction worsening as a result. Or will a seismically massive social change fundamentally occur through some future much needed paradigm shift in sociocultural perspectives and political attitudes towards addiction preventative social policy legislation?

Nevertheless drug abuse images in the mass media create a situation of a socio-stratified labelling, producing self-fulfilling 'lifeworld' prophecies and symptomatic social problems on a monumentally epic scale. An international social crisis which the drug user dreams will shift from analysing individual potential and intellectual worth in such a way as that media bipolarity of analysis will one day champion the benefits of psychoactive substances, and not vilify the plight of the victims of drug addiction.

The depths of the causation determinism to which the individuals involved in drug abuse culture, especially the youth, disadvantaged poor, the underclasses and future younger generations are influenced by the portrayal of the mass media archetypes of power, influence and wealth; represented by users, addict's, gang culture and drug dealers in the cultural consciousness. Reaching its concluding pinnacle summit through label internalisations manifesting the 'self-fulfilling prophecy' of becoming either drug abuse victims, drug dealers or gang overlords who through their operational realities perpetuate the global socioeconomic inequalities and cultural deprivation that they as individuals have socially overcome, passed on in a new cultural form of existential realism to future generations.

Ultimately it is the systemic cultural inequalities of opinionated social inequity and inequality, passed on through the labelling process of social interaction that is enforced on the subordinated weaker individual by those with authority and power which produces these 'self-fulfilling prophecies' of negative inner city gang subculture. A social reality which is often hard, gritty and unnecessarily violent and oppressive to the individuals concerned, a subculture which is also subsequently and inherently fueled by the individual desire for, and social availability of, illegal illicit psychoactive substances.

A society of inherent recreational substance abuse that is represented in multiple perspectives of cultural illumination; as both a collection of cultural problems and as a cluster of social opportunities. As a social problem in the newspaper publications whose existence will only cessate through the elite introducing tougher enforcement measures, harsher penalties for individual drug users and through reducing the personal freedoms and human rights that we all enjoy as the intellectual foundation of our positively emancipated empowerment through realised individuality. The fundamental dynamic of social and cultural existence as our way of life, that the socially legitimating political powers and opinion determining policy makers of the economic and political elites would all too easily lead us to question as worthwhile and would insist is a blockade to the route to progress, the progress of their lust for absolute power over our love of true freedom.

But drug use as I mentioned is also represented in its logical antithesis to the realist rationalisation of a social problem, as the cultural representation in the mass media of gang subculture as an essential mirror image to the sociocultural motivation towards a progressive realisation of individual freedoms, love and personal liberty. This is due to the fact that illegal drug gang culture is culturally represented at the same time as a social problem as the cultural representation of achievable and realistically 'illegitimate opportunity structure' of viable potential opportunity for an individual to aspire to, in the progressive self-actualisation of their personal desire for self-achievement in the economic and social hierarchies of power, wealth and influence; through participation in the operating underground 'black market economies', contained within the fluctuating balance of the international existential geopolitical realities. Falsely portrayed as the fundamental foundation for a social agency of cultural change, for the majority of the truly poor, whose life opportunities have been stifled and restrained by a state of social, political and economic inequality, perpetuated by those whose cultural opulence and privilege favours the elite few already possessed of such a social existence, at the expense vast majority of everybody else, deemed less fortunate than their elitist brethren through their unprivileged social status.

This creates within our cultural consensus conglomeration of existential social realities a self-perpetuating system of cyclic cultural causation determined by individual socioeconomic inequalities. Through the personally learned symbolism of our individual 'lifeworld' interactions, where conceptual meanings, empathic inclinations, intellectual thoughts and the theoretical origin of all human cultural existential realities originate and operate within their zones of influence.

Where the 'lifeworld' situation inherited by the underclass finds its cultural development, initially through a sociological understanding of our existential nature, but only when it is applied without the introspective developments to the awareness and capacities of our natural psychology, in the comprehension of the social reality of our existence, the understandings are limited to the paradigm of criminology, as all that the individual can gleen of the wisdoms and knowledge, evident in the engendered social activities, demonstrated by the United Kingdom underclass riots of early (2010). Since then the revolutionary potential of the underclasses cultural consciousness as represents the apex agency of gang culture, it is limited to the realisations of its capacity for flash-lightning violence and prolific drug abuse of existential social reality criminalities, and not the force for cultural and social change that many drug users believe it is, or wish it could become.

As we are hereby hence launching the investigation into the criminal downfall of our society and of our very way life in its distinctive features and cultural existence, through the conflictual and dichotomous over-representation of drug use and addiction in the mass-media and definitive presentation the intricate nature of the underground operation of the 'illegitimate opportunity structures' which constitute the international 'black market economies' of the illegal drug trade industry, we have to ask; what could a speculative future human perspective yield for worthy possibilities of a social policy and a recreational cultural existence be for future generations. An illegal and subversive industry which I believe if was made legitimate through the legalisation of novel psychoactive substances, would earn the government billions upon billions in tax and international trade, making the users of such compounds safer and happier in their social prospects and life potential that can be actualised.

That for the sake of the individual drug users enjoying themselves and actually having a good time, they can do so knowing they are not running the potential risk of going to prison and being forced into social confinement, mixing for years in an enclosed and restricted insular environment with the most sinister and dangerous members of our society; the rapists, kidnappers, torturers and murderers who are isolated and imprisoned for our safety, because they literally represent such a level of risk to us.

Yet the social extent to which these social 'illegitimate opportunity structures' operate is paralleled by the influences upon the individual originating in the music industry and the culture of gang warfare and drug culture in the celebrity exhalation to the ranks of cultural elite stardom of a few members of such drug culture heroes. The 'war on drugs' however is a social war and not a cultural one, criminality is an objective social definition of deviance from the normally accepted mode of conduct which is the the law, not just as a cultural definition of deviance through personal difference in the ideals of our life aims and the values which guide us in our life choices, which are freely selected and eclectically chosen by us as individuals, representing our own unique perspectives developed through exercising our personal freedom, experience, life aim and, social goals for ourselves and others, which are enshrined through exercising our democratic freedom of choice, civil liberty and our human rights.

But as long as drug culture and drug abuse is considered a social issue and is labelled as criminal, and is forced underground into the operation of the 'black market economies' illicit substances 'illegitimate opportunity structures' these will represent to the economically underprivileged individuals, who have no current capacity for upward social mobility in their current lives, or their foreseeable futures a means of gain. These cross-stratification organisations in the social body offer the individual user an opportunity to essentially 'level up' in the in the cultural, economic and political hierarchy of the worldwide illegal drug trade of the 'black market economy' to gain the substantial increase and achievement of money, wealth, fame, respect, influence and power, which is so persuasively endorsed by these sub-culturally originating celebrities through the greater cultural representation of the underclasses that they represent through the cultural reinforcement of the mass-media music culture industry.

But with the 'gang-star' subcultural heroes living in excessive social and cultural opulence, with endless numbers of status symbols and money in their bank accounts; the massive mansions, numerous sports cars, luxury fine living and expensive jet-set holidays are glorified in their rise to power from their underground drug-dealing underclass days to the current celebrity status of their personal story of aspiration, ambition and self-actualisation up the stratified social hierarchy of the culture industry. Exemplified through the mass media in the rise and fall of artists and record label owners like the once notorious Shug Knight of Death Row Records, whose dealings ended their careers when the hood attitude prevailed at the top of the industry itself and murdered fellow stars Tupac Shakur & Biggie Smalls before their time, Kading, G., (2011).

These 'rags to riches' stories represent a perception of cultural legitimation and belief consensus to the ideologically structured categorical opinionation of both the mass-media consumer individual drug user addict's and dealers on the 'street level' of the economic social structure, who fuel the illegal black market drug economy that sometimes 'crime pays'. That drug users and dealers (who are almost always users themselves) whose personal traumas and damaged psychological dispositional, alleviated through substance use and reinforced through the labelling processes of subcultural socialisation and introspective objectification through their self-image fulfilling prophecy determinism, can if not achieve in their futures what their popular heroes have achieved, then can at least believe that one day they can; the origins of modern day 'false consciousness' through the literal 'opium of the people', Marx, K., & Engels, F., (1846).

The social theorist of state propaganda and mass-media manipulation Antonio Gramsci introduced the concept of Hegemony to the subject of Sociology, when in field of culture, deviance and social control, the upper class ecopolitical elite of society, represent through the mass media culture industry apparatus their and only their ontological perspectives. That the opulent and decadent lifestyles of wealth, power, money, fame, influence and personal glory is the only socially acceptable and culturally legitimate lifestyle and individual career goal worthy of either serious social ambition or genuine personal aspiration.

Hence the only true moral values and cultural beliefs worth having in our ideological makeup and actual meanings that we develop in our opinions that are worth pursuing as conceptual definitions of the objective existential representations of factual reality in our attitudes towards ourselves and each other, are displaced outside of their actual manifest effective causation. And the reason why: For the sake of an unstoppable rampaging sense of superficial pleasure and satisfaction in the construct of the self through the 'intravenous opium of the people' that is the mass-media lifestyle promoted by the culture industry. Adorno, T.W., (1991)

The reason why? Because the opinion brokers and watchdog gatekeepers of the mass-media culture industry offer it to us, just like the drug pusher of the street gangs selling heroin, to try to alleviate their own overwhelming despair in the face of the many problems of a broken global system, one which still ultimately fails to provide any true or real answers or effective solutions to the many social illnesses and cultural problems that, as we blot the sun from the sky in pursuit of an irradiating superficial satisfaction. One to dull our senses to the woes of the human condition, and reduce through hedonistic compulsion our enlightened few moments to ourselves become the slaves of selfish and economically obsessed gluttony of visceral self-gratification as the perpetual free choosing consumers of constant repeated effluence over a unique and rare inspiring affluence.

So in the progressively united and globalised world in which we live, we see the elite black market world suppliers and exporters, of the countries of origin where the drugs are exported from one dock and are imported through another, with each link operating in the drug supply chain through its individual causal determinism. Each time in a constant ebb and flow of ships on trade routes, into and out of major ports and cities according to the mapped global trade routes, each individual in the process of the drug economies connective linkage each time a transaction is processed and fulfilled, becomes more powerful and wealthy as a result.

This is where the illegitimate opportunity structures at work in culture and on the streets in gang culture and the British society grow beyond all borders infecting every nation across the world through the elites inability to effectively deal with a burgeoning growing international social problem through profound incompetence and stunning inferiority to rise to the occasion and be true leaders of society.

But the problem is not with an elite having dominance or control in our society, for any society must have an elite in order for it to run and function successfully. But elite decadence for example is where we see politicians syphoning off public funds for their privileged private personal business ventures to the crumbling of the state and stability of the global world economy. Also we see elite decadence presented in the mass media culture industry represented as our embellished societal norms and cultural values. That their lifestyle of money, fame and power is the only truly worthwhile way to live and to have money is the only object of true value in its literal sense, this is superficial infatuation and obsession instigating our interpersonal decadence and social ignorance as legitimate ethical and social norms and values in our current stagnated cultural climate today, Althusser (1970).

So naturally this cultural situation produces ideological dissonance in society, usually at the bottom end of the scale where the people who take the drugs do not believe in the decadence of the elitist rich, who try to form an effective counter culture, from which you can reconsider everything and most importantly the drug laws.

This cultural revolutionary potential for agency seen in the psychoactive proliferation movement of the 1960's shows the potential for cultural action towards a social consensus of possession decriminalisation and a progressive social policy legalisation at its heart embodying the attitudes of informed free choice and liberal utilitarianism. For such a cultural milu of change that championed individual knowledge over social ignorance would indeed enable the individual drug user to live a life that would not incur the personal life chance altering negativities such as criminalisation and incarceration for the sake of either having a good time or opening your mind, if this were so it would shift the mainstream media opinions to the tenets of the modern counterculture movement itself.

Counterculture today that is heavily drawn upon drug experience, from the LSD 'hippies' of the 1960's, the Magic Mushrooms of the 1950's 'teddy boys' the Amphetamines riots of the 'mod's' and the 'rocker's' of the 1960s and 70s, or MDMA 'ravers' of the 1990's, counterculture has always involved some from of illicit drug use and the subsequent expression in an artistic form of the enlightenment that the compound innately possesses in its shamanic psychology. Therefore, in as much as drug use has always been inherent to the paradigm shift advancement of spiritual consciousness and cultural perspectives, in some form drug culture and use is inevitably and unequivocally sure to continue, the question is this; with the development of Novel Psychoactive Substances, can the future of drug use be made safer for those who partake? The answer is most definitely yes, though revolutionary new social policy legislation and mainstream cultural legitimation, with individual and subcultural insight to lead the way forward, into a future where the exploration of self and consciousness, is an undeniable and fundamental part of our human sociocultural and psychospiritual existential natural progression.

The need for new groundbreaking perspectives towards future drug decriminalisation and legalisation as a cultural movement originates in the musical and literary subcultural and countercultural underground, this is because of the generated mass-media dissonance and inherent discord created by the bilateral polemic dichotomy of inherently conflictual cultural and social tangents of paradigm progression, being woven into the same manifesting collective sociocultural tangent. The progression of the 'war on drugs' 'moral panic' will only have the effect of forcing drug use and users into a more subversive and dangerous social existence, and create a darker pseudo-consensus for all through a false mainstream reflexive perceptual cultural reflection of the actual and true individual normalities and 'lifeworld' realities that pervade our societies organisation. As newly developing perspectives slowly emerge among the disempowered social groups of associating divergent youth and individuals, new norms and values will find expression their new norms and values of subculture, through the new symbolic meanings and subcultural codes of fashions, styles, concepts, visions, ideals, hopes, dress codes, beliefs, technologies, artefacts and all creative personal significations and manifestations to be found within the individual realisation of that future subcultural lifestyle which so becomes the novel and new norm.

The question as to what extent the in future humanity will of resolved the social dissonance which so exists for us today in the form of the illegality of drug use and it's conflictual social and cultural elements and to what extent and to what extent the intellectual reasoning and creative artistic intelligence in prevalent attitudes of subcultural drug counterculture in the revolutionary lower tiers and underclasses of society have their political efficacy and effectiveness remains to be answered. When the sociopolitical economically empowered elite rule from the apex top in a polarisation resembling both an ivory-tower and underground bunker of perpetual moral decay and cultural stagnation simultaneously, through overvaluing their status symbols, their power base and the true worth of all their statistical wealth the fate of the future drug user is as of yet an undetermined destiny.

I suppose that the answer to the previous question boils down to the further question: To what extent can progressive drug laws and the perspectives of drug use counterculture come to be represented in a positive light by the culture industry and mass media in the future? For progressive drug use social policy to become prevalent in the minds, attitudes and thoughts of the politicians who decide upon its introduction in the future the sociopolitical polarisation of the issue depends upon the people being most affected by it, the individual drug users, have their perspectives and opinions elevated to a position of power in social, cultural and political circles of representation and influence with liberal egalitarian clarity not political popularity, in order to make progressive changes to current social policy and directly influence changes to the drug laws, Husak (2002).

When a drug is decriminalised it is not to say that it is considered as culturally acceptable behaviour, nor is it ingratiate in the consensus of the social theory of the public body, as there are still concerns as to the overall perception of the projected consequences to the introduction of pro-drug liberal policy. Personally, the right to take a drug means that in order to have the right to take any drug depends on the need, and choice of the drug taker, and not society in its nature. But if the drug is safer to take, it merely means that the social fallout or negativity that is caused by the taking of the drug to society, is of such a nature that the needs of the user are taken care of so that the manifest consequent ripple effect is not one of the issues.

This requires the change of sociopolitical policy legislation perspective, or else drug use and drug culture is forced further underground, and the negative social and personal fallout from drug use becomes more secretive and dangerous, increasing risk exponentially with its marginalisation and criminalisation in the public eye. Only when a drug has been decriminalised in a specific township or city area can the rehabilitation of the people in that area who use a drug but suffer unnecessary risk and problems of that use really begin to rehabilitate. This has been shown by Glasgow City Council in (2017) where heroin users instead of being arrested, convicted, given a criminal record and sent to a detention centre for 10-years for basically healing their chronic psychological or physiological pain.

The right not to suffer is fundamental, feeling like the realities of their life have destroyed them in a universe which has been brutally unfair and against them, is, fundamentally, mental pain. So rehabilitate these poor individuals who have been already unfairly treated so badly, traumatised and emotionally destroyed, on so many levels, so they need not be subject to further barbarism in life. Through being arrested and sent to prison and having all civil liberties taken away from them; for only through the socially responsible policy of drug use decriminalisation can rehabilitation truly begin to occur.

All illegal street drugs have legitimate medical uses, from opiates and cocaine derivatives been used as painkillers in the hospital setting and in dentistry surgical procedures, to potentially healing the mind through the more exotic stimulation techniques and psychoactive based remedy, as Magic Mushrooms, LSD and enhancers such as amphetamine which has been used in the military since the day it was invented. Ecstasy and magic mushrooms have massive therapeutic benefits in mental health studies, psychology, psychotherapy, psychiatry and counselling. I shall look at some of the more legitimate spiritual uses of drugs in my conclusion; but for now I've discussed this point enough, see Huxley (1956).

So the penalty for possession of drugs may differ between countries, such as in Amsterdam and Cuba where the removal of such penal penalty, through cultural legitimation sees both personal and social empath utilitarianism. We see the legitimate use of drugs in a clinical setting abroad already, why not also as a way of personal enjoyment and recreational activity in a new cultural paradigm shift in drug policy to incorporate the fact that alcohol and nicotine are drugs, and therefore should we not consider what the benefits of each drug, before we ban them. There are other drugs besides alcohol and nicotine that serve recreational social and personal psychological purposes?

But because drug use will always have negative factors as well, we must compensate for this, we must balance the factors with the tax earned from sale in shops. Through tax and with the wise spending of it and progressive social drug policy, these two factors, can neutralise the social fallout accountable for the social issue and effectively counterbalance the interaction in the negative effects upon individuals.

So this leads us down the lines of causation that drugs can be used to alleviate individual negative and unfortunate life situations, achieve personal recreational enjoyment achieving a feeling of satisfaction after a hard day's work or for personal psychological and spiritual exploration as well. Indeed in the creating and producing of a state of mind through a materialist biochemical trigger, our personal empowerment through drugs is limitless. The personal experience of the user is the alchemical elixir, from healing through just having a good time or for personal growth through the expansion of consciousness, in itself self seeks to be transformed and alchemized into the product of the new form of self culture; to achieve enlightenment and inspire others to aspire.

But whilst the individual and society are under the effects of the 'moral panic' visual and cultural representation of liberial drugs policy will always be negative, protecting against the downfall of social standards is through legitimisation and legalisation. But change seems a long way off the horizon to becoming an actual lifeworld reality until now.

In the far off future the attitudes and personal reasons people do the drugs in the first place, will have seen positive change. And in such an era of personal, social and cultural empowerment its fundamental nature will be radically different to the 'illegitimate opportunity structures' operating. The drug gang lifestyle, glorified in mass media representations we see in the music and culture industry today, will change to liberal eclectic self signification of individual uniqueness and character not the false virtues of money, wealth and power.

A shift away from glorified drug dealers and organised social conflict, towards spiritual and emotional empowerment and perceptual and personal development, would perhaps make the drug takers of tomorrow, be able to make more of their lives than simply becoming dealers, addicts or overlords. To put simply the individual is free to enjoy the benefits of social recreational drug use, instead of suffering habitual subcultural drug addiction and abuse.

To take recreational psychoactive substances in a moral way, to sculpt ourselves at the subconscious level of the labelling process, images and mental emotional will, in the image of our own ideals, inspirations and sculpt their true self and truest aspiration in transformed form. Then take personal experience into the future representation of self and culture. As what individuals themselves produce as artists, scientists, musicians and philosophers of tomorrow.

Perhaps the positive empowering energy of enlightenment is the essence where the ideal of true equality among people could come from in my opinion, as a real consideration and thought for the possibility of egalitarian nature and moral standing as an existential construct. For why when we can see, why would we want to be a superficial representation of something which is essentially negative and not in all our best interests. We may, with a shift in cultural paradigms, see a shift to seek to become something which is positive, and in everyone's best interest representing that which is truly the nature of positive egalitarian liberal philosophy.

So perhaps this in itself would become the basis for the start of a social and cultural era of progress and self betterment occuring. The beginning of the Neomodernist era after the end of the second world war, only unlike in the second world war, in the post-war era where we were trying to create better than the horrors which we had experienced in war.

Maybe then politicians will be pragmatic enough to take the not quite so horrible, but not quite so incredible, starting base of our society, and seek to make it better. Not the aspirations of youth recoiling from horror, but out of aspiring for something more than just what we have inherited from the previous generations.

This comes nearly to my concluding point, that the utopian ideal society, where we all can have a positive state of existence, where all negative social fallout; personal, psychological, cultural or of a mental health level. Drug use can be empathetic and empathic counterbalanced or accommodated for, through the effective use of spending capital and tax not on weapons of war, and restrictive enforcement measures, Taylor (1982). But money spent on hospitals, healthcare, emergency services, education and new social institutions, would aim at taking individuals and making them turn into everything in life, becoming all that they can possibly be, and achieve and can possibly become; the essential crux of the Psychoanalytical work of Maslow (1939).

Conclusion:

The factors for analysis in my concluding question remain as they have been throughout the study as I ask: what would happen if not only the once called 'legal highs' but all recreational drugs, were legalised at some point in the future? The first thing to be noted, is that the Edinburgh City Council's policy decision of the decriminalisation of heroin, resulting in a monumental drop in all crime and drug related crime is evidence that liberal minded social policy is more effective than any punitive measure.

Another thing which should be noted is that the black market maintenance of illegitimate opportunity structures in the underground illegal drug economy would effectively bottom out and cease to be a viable source of capital, collapsing as the main source of income for the black market. No longer an influx of money into the underground criminal organised crime syndicate social structures which exist, crime rates would drop to unprecedented levels ensuring a better quality of life for all individuals in society.

Another thing which could be considered as fundamental is that through recreational drug use being legalised a cultural shift and change of personal focus from inclusion in the fundamental power play based drug dealing gang culture and a victim based drug taking underclass could come to be. A liberal and empathetic development of an individual's psychological development and creative personal understanding of introspective knowledge through the psychedelic exploration of one's connection to their soul, spirit, heart and mind.

Through the recreational psychological enhancement and creative stimulation and activation of the subconscious mind, through psychedelic augmentation and enablement of one's intellectual and perceptual knowledge can become possible. A new awareness and paradigm of knowledge of our self-consciousness through a psychedelic cultural movement within the potential vision of the future generations may become a social and cultural prescient of realised personal value and achievable self actualisation.

But as long as the mass-media controls the prevalent generalisations and objectification of acceptable popular opinions and the policy determining causations of political influence through such false consensus our social progress is inherently going to be stifled. The social and cultural mechanics of the dominant thoughts of our society limit these progressive and positive dreams and aspirations to be but pipedreams and diversions from the accepted norm.

So to further explore this potential for change, if illegal drugs were legalised beyond the scope of the current Misuse of Drugs Act's A, B, and C stratification system of recreational drug categorisation, and be replaced with a new system, what would this system of the future look like?

There are certain fundamental considerations for such a system to exist as a prevention against drug abuse and fatality, which are the danger and toxicity, addiction of a substance and the dependence values and scales used in drug classification must be included. Individuals would therefore be tested for allergy and intolerance to these psychoactive recreational substances and medicines to expose any prevalent physiological sensitivities and dangerous factors. These would be kept on a purchasing card and displayed to the supplying pharmacist on a microchip and on the front individual's card in the form of a sweat sensitive reader, in order to not compromise the individuals safety whilst taking recreational psychoactive compounds.

The card issued for the purchasing of these compounds at pharmacies would have incorporated in it a biometric data reading sweat sensitive square that contains physiologically dependent drug intoxication level and tolerance level results analysis data on the chip. This is so the individual would not be able to purchase any more of the said intoxicating compounds and the contraindicating substance use toxiological effects upon their physiological genetic constitution which could expose them to a risk of an overdose or excessive damage through compound toxicity.

On a cultural level the late Victorian utilitarian and libertarian philosopher John Stuart Mill, primarily associated with the groundbreaking work On Liberty, discusses the fundamental hedonic nature of higher and lower pleasures of self, spirit, body and mind. In the piece of literature he defines the higher pleasures of spiritual perception and esoteric experience as the highest form of pleasure, and lays out that the formulation the closest experience an individual can achieve, but even is by itself hard to achieve, is the end result of self actualisation through spiritual enlightenment, Mill, J.S. (1859).

The higher pleasure of intellectual thought and subconscious perceptual desublimation he describes as the second-highest fundamental essence of pleasure that a human individual is capable of experiencing. Achievable through rigorous philosophical thought, mental training and intellectual study, but also can be gleaned at and momentarily comprehended through introspectively directed exploration of the self through recreational drug use; where one can elevate the mind to experience the enlightenment and euphoria of emotional emancipation and social connection to others through the empowering alignment of social empathy and psychological intuition.

The basis for the comparison between the two is that he believes that in order to experience the wonder of true spiritual pleasure and become enlightened, you must first understand your inner self and nature. Through opening your mind to higher levels of conscious reality, which are what define higher pleasures in their fundamental nature, he believes that through drugs you can unlock this unique higher potential of humanity.

The 16th century philosophy of the French theologian and rationalist philosopher Rene Descartes in his intellectual milestone piece of literature Meditations On First Philosophy, describes the function of the Pineal Gland in the human brains complex neuroanatomy as the matter-energy 'nexus' between the physical (corporeal) and mental (divine) stratified fundamental dimensions of experiential human reality, Descartes, R. (1641)

It has since been discovered by psychologists and neurologists doing research in recent years that the Pineal Gland appears to synthesise dimethyltryptamine or DMT as it is known in popular literature of recreational drug culture and spiritual special interest groups, Axelrod, J. & Fraschini, F., (2013). DMT is known to have a greater binding efficacy to a factor of eight in the primary neural-receptor synaptic clefts of the neurons in the frontal lobes than the standard binding endocrine neurochemical serotonin for those cortical areas; from which DMT is also synthesised out of in the Pineal Gland, when the molecule is in its most abundant levels of synaptic saturation. This means that the presence of DMT, albeit naturally through Pineal endocrine synthesis or through ingestion from a psychoactive substance, causes a hyperactive modus operandi of frontal lobe neural functioning to kick into effect.

As such it has since the original philosophical formulation of Descartes also been discovered in recent years that the Pineal Gland in humans also contains photoreceptor cells, albeit of a different fundamental configuration of electromagnetic spectral perceptual nature to the ones in the retina of the eye. These photoreceptor cells are fundamentally designed for detection of the pervasive and tissue penetrative wavelengths of the spectrum of the human electromagnetic aura, or human spiritual energy field. This hints at a possible reconciliation between the theoretical, intellectual and scientific paradigms of the spiritual, religious, psychic, psychiatric, psychological, and philosophical fields of academic study and pursuit.

Bearing these two philosophical thinkers in mind it really does lead to consideration of a great cultural potential for much more successful consideration and speculation as for what liberal drug culture could look like and become in the future. A socially legitimate way of life through genuine informed and liberated cultural consensus under the banner of liberal and progressive drug policies to be adopted in the future.

As such the future of culturally accepted options upon recreational drug use and socially conceived attitudes towards future drug policy should focus on successfully informing citizens of all the facts and inherent risks involved in pursuing recreational drug use and taking psychoactive substances. This is due to the fact that as well as having innate associated risks, all illegal drugs have both positive and beneficial legitimate medical and psychotherapeutic uses inherent to their physiological functions and underlying mechanisms of action.

Due to the fact that informed individuals are more likely to make wise beneficial decisions and are less likely to make foolish or risk involving decisions in their future, the issue as for how to be effective in preventing individuals from enduring the risks of drug abuse is self inherent. More than relying upon penal punishment as a measure of social control that through enabling the individuals own free will as the mechanism of action, taking its greatest effect on their manifest choices and their social behaviours ro be of a more aware and fundamentally enlightened human being is key.

So a final point for the successful introduction of new social policy to bring about a reduction of crime in inner-city areas really has to be that of the liberal and culturally progressive drug decriminalisation and legalisation policy implementation, so that recreational users are treated well and accommodated for in society. The policy for the decriminalisation of heroin in Edinburgh in the year of was a massive success and statistically it has seen a landmark drop in all crime, not just drug related, across the entire statistical cross-sectional range of recorded demographically considered data.

My final point for this research article is to recommend that all illegal recreational drugs and psychoactive compounds be first decriminalised as to reduce the risks involved to the individual and to protect against the potential of incurred harm through criminal consequences. Then society should consider looking towards a process of true legalisation so that informed individuals can make their own choices and not have any decisions made for them by a dominating propagandistic 'war on drugs' elitist agenda of the draconian and authoritarian hegemonic interest, of a mass media controlling social consensus and policy manipulating definition of what we individually consider is both acceptable and truly legitimate personal and social behaviour.

Bibliography:

Adamson, W.L., (2014) Hegemony & Revolution: Antonio Gramsci's Political & Cultural Theory. Echo Point: New York.

Adorno, T.W., (1991) The Culture Industry: Selected Essays On Mass Culture. Routledge: London.

Althusser, L. (1970) Ideology & Ideological State Apparatuses. Verso: London.

Axelrod, J. & Fraschini, F., (2013) Pineal Gland & It's Endocrine Role. Springer: London.

Becker, H.S., (1963) *Outsiders*, Free Press: New York.

Cloward, R., & Ohlin L., (1960) *Illegitimate Opportunity Structures*. Free Press: New York.

Cohen, A.K., (1955) *Delinquent Boys: The Culture of The Gang*. Free Press: Illinois.

Cohen, S., (1974) *Folk Devil's and Moral Panics*. Routledge: London.

Comte, A (1865) A General View Of Positivism. Kessinger Publishing: London.

Descartes, R. (1641) *Meditations On First Philosophy*. Routledge: London.

Durkheim, E. (1897) Suicide. Free Press: New York.

Frazier, E.F. (1957) *The Black Bourgeoisie*. Free Press: New York.

Garfoot, A.P. (2010) *Dawn of The Neomodern: Art, Humanism & The Meme*. Lulu Press: London.

Goode, E., & Ben-Yehuda, N., (1994) *Moral Panics: The Social Construction of Deviance*. Hoboken: New Jersey.

Gramsci, A., (1947) Selections From The Prison Notebooks. International Publishers: London.

Husak, D. (2002) Legalise This!. Verso Books: London.

Huxley, A. (1956) The Doors Of Perception. Harper Perennial Modern Classics: New York.

Lyotard, J.F., (1979) The Postmodern Condition: A Report On Knowledge. Manchester University Press: Manchester.

Marx, K., & Engels, F., (1846) The German Ideology. Prometheus Books: London.

Maslow, A.H., (1943). "A theory of human motivation". Psychological Review. 50 (4): 370–396.

Kading, G., (2011) Murder Rap: The Untold Story of the Biggie Smalls & Tupac Shakur Murder Investigations by the Detective Who Solved Both Cases. One Time Publishing: New York.

Mead, G.H. (1934) *Mind, Self & Society*. Hackett: Illinois.

Merton, R.K., (1938) Social Theory & Social Structure. The Free Press: New York.

Merton: R.K. (1996) *On Social Structure & Science*. University of Chicago Press: Chicago.

Mill, J.S. (1859) *On Liberty*. Longman, Roberts & Green: London.

Miller, W. (1959) "*Lower Class Culture A Generating Milieu of Gang Delinquency*" Journal Of Social Issues: 14 (3): 5-20.

Miller, W., (1959) "*Implications of Urban Lower Class Culture For Social Work.*" Social Service Review 33 (3): 219-236.

Moreland, R.L., & Levine, J.M., (1982) "*Socialisation In Small Groups: Temporal Changes In Individual-Group Relations.*" Advances In Experimental Social Psychology. [Vol 15 pp. 137-192]

Nixon, R. (1971) *Presidential Press Conference.* The White House: Washington.

Tannenbaum, F., (1938) *Crime & Community.* Columbia University Press: New York.

Taylor, K. (1982) Political Ideas of The Utopian Socialists. Routledge: London.

Thrasher F.T., (1927) *The Gang.* Chicago University Press: Chicago.

The Global Commission on Drug Policy. (2011) p. 24.

Willis, P.E., (1977) Learning To Labour: How Working Class Kids Get Working Class Jobs. Routledge: London.

Online News Article References:

Accessed: 7/12/2022: 3pm-6pm

1. https://www.bbc.co.uk/news/uk-england-cornwall-17843087

2. https://www.bbc.co.uk/news/uk-scotland-glasgow-west-19046525

3. https://www.bbc.co.uk/news/uk-wales-south-west-wales-21671726

4. https://www.bbc.co.uk/news/world-europe-22697505

5. https://www.bbc.co.uk/news/uk-politics-22771232

6. https://www.bbc.co.uk/news/world-europe-23058289

7. https://www.bbc.co.uk/news/uk-23048267

8. https://www.bbc.co.uk/news/uk-england-24128315

9. https://www.bbc.co.uk/news/health-26089126

10. https://www.bbc.co.uk/news/newsbeat-27487942

11. https://www.bbc.co.uk/news/newsbeat-30878532

12. https://www.bbc.co.uk/news/newsbeat-31599506

13. https://www.bbc.co.uk/news/uk-england-34603665

14. https://www.bbc.co.uk/news/uk-england-35173915

15. https://www.bbc.co.uk/news/uk-northern-ireland-36037173

16. https://www.bbc.co.uk/news/av/uk-england-36257218

17. https://www.bbc.co.uk/news/uk-scotland-36278908

18. https://www.bbc.co.uk/news/uk-36280501

19. https://www.bbc.co.uk/news/uk-england-manchester-36387992

20. https://www.bbc.co.uk/news/uk-england-london-37166003

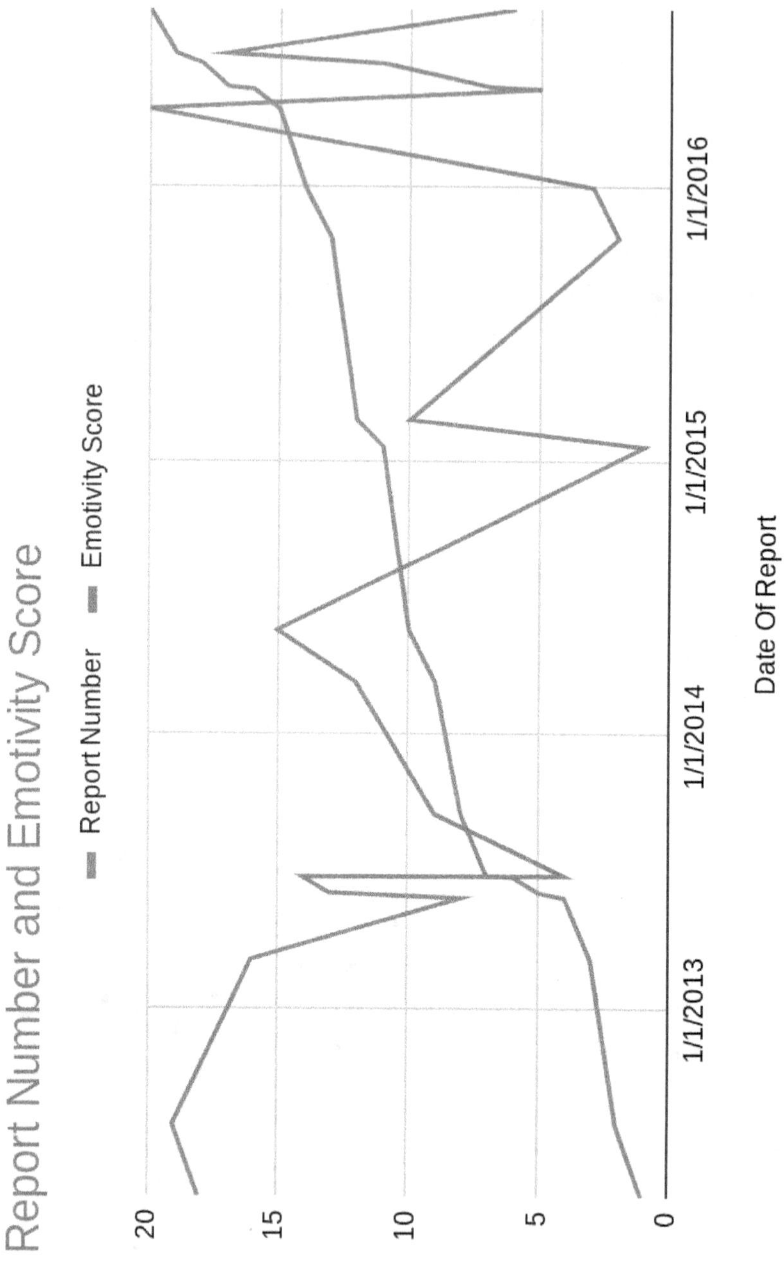

Report Number and Emotivity Score

Report Number ▬ Emotivity Score ▬

20

15

10

5

0

1/1/2013   1/1/2014   1/1/2015   1/1/2016

Date Of Report

Data Table Of Results

Report Number	Date Of Report	Emotive Words	Total Words	Emotivity Ratio	Emotivity Score	Commentary
1	25/4/2012	9	148	16.44	18	Police Officials
2	30/07/2012	24	354	14.75	19	Paramedics
3	7/3/2013	19	333	17.52	16	Psychiatrist
4	28/5/2013	13	417	29.78	8	EMCDDA
5	4/6/2013	10	255	25.5	13	Home Office Minister
6	25/6/2013	11	272	24.72	14	OUODC
7	26/6/2013	18	681	37.83	4	UNODC
8	17/9/2013	10	281	28.1	9	Director Of Public Health
9	12/3/2014	29	775	26.72	12	-
10	20/5/2014	24	593	24.7	15	Police Officials
11	19/1/2015	19	940	49.47	1	Police Officials
12	24/2/2015	27	741	27.44	10	Police Officials
13	24/10/2015	16	699	43.68	2	Paramedics
14	31/12/2015	12	436	36.33	3	Paramedics
15	13/4/2016	32	420	13.12	20	-
16	10/5/2016	2	67	33.5	5	-
17	13/5/2016	28	820	29.28	7	-
18	13/6/2016	43	1160	26.97	11	-
19	26/6/2016	11	185	16.81	17	-
20	24/8/2016	10	307	30.76	6	-

www.ingramcontent.com/pod-product-compliance
Lightning Source LLC
Chambersburg PA
CBHW060340290526
45793CB00003B/675